Australia

Travel Guide

2024-2025

Discover Top Destinations, Hidden Gems, Local Culture, Adventure Activities, and Essential Travel Tips for an Unforgettable Aussie Experience

By
Alex J. Holden

Table Of Contents

Chapter 1

Australia at a Glance

Australia is a land like no other, with vast landscapes that stretch across sun-baked deserts, tropical rainforests, and snow-capped mountains. It is a country of staggering natural beauty, where world-famous icons like the Great Barrier Reef and Uluru are matched by the sheer diversity of its regions, wildlife, and cultural heritage. As the world's sixth-largest country and the only one to occupy an entire continent, Australia boasts an unparalleled combination of vibrant cities, remote outback areas, and pristine coastal escapes.

The country's vibrant cities—Sydney, Melbourne, Brisbane, Perth, and Adelaide—are cosmopolitan hubs brimming with energy, creativity, and culture. They are known for their iconic landmarks, cutting-edge architecture, and stunning harbors, yet each city offers something unique. Sydney, for example, is famous for its dazzling harbor and the Sydney Opera House, while Melbourne is renowned for its thriving arts scene, eclectic food culture, and laneway cafes. Perth, located on the west coast, combines natural beauty with urban sophistication, while Brisbane and Adelaide offer subtropical warmth and a laid-back, welcoming atmosphere.

Yet, beyond the cities lies a sprawling countryside of breathtaking diversity. From the wild outback of the Northern Territory and the ancient red landscapes of Western Australia to the lush vineyards of South Australia and the spectacular Great Ocean Road in Victoria, Australia invites exploration in every corner. The coastline alone, stretching over 25,000 kilometers, is lined with some of the world's best beaches—Bondi Beach, Whitehaven Beach, and Cable Beach are just the beginning of Australia's extraordinary coastal offerings.

In addition to its scenic beauty, Australia is celebrated for its unique wildlife. It is one of the few places on Earth where you can encounter iconic species such as kangaroos, koalas, wombats, and platypuses in their natural habitats. Australia's isolation has led to the evolution of a wide range of flora and fauna, with over 80% of its plants, mammals, and reptiles found nowhere else in the world. Whether you're exploring the coastal bushlands, the lush rainforests of Queensland, or the arid deserts of the Red Centre, the chance to spot rare wildlife will undoubtedly be a highlight of your trip.

Australia is made up of six states and two territories, each offering its own distinct experiences. New South Wales, home to Sydney and the famous Blue Mountains, contrasts with the rugged beauty of Tasmania, an island state filled with wild nature reserves and rich colonial history. Queensland is famed for its year-round tropical weather and the Great Barrier Reef, while Victoria and South Australia are cultural powerhouses, boasting fine wine regions and world-class museums. The Northern Territory is where travelers can experience the Australian outback in its most authentic form, including visiting the awe-inspiring Uluru, one of Australia's most sacred indigenous sites. Western Australia, the largest state, offers travelers vast stretches of untouched wilderness, including stunning national parks and pristine beaches along its Coral Coast.

Australia's story is rooted in one of the oldest continuous cultures in the world. The country's indigenous heritage spans tens of thousands of years, with Aboriginal and Torres Strait Islander peoples having cultivated deep connections to the land, sea, and sky. The Dreamtime stories, passed down through generations, offer insights into their spiritual beliefs and connection to nature. Today, there are many opportunities for travelers to respectfully engage with indigenous culture—whether it's through art, storytelling, or participating in cultural tours, Australia's indigenous heritage is an integral part of the nation's identity.

Modern Australia, while young in terms of European settlement, is a thriving multicultural society that prides itself on openness and diversity. Australians are known for their friendly and easygoing nature, and their love of the outdoors is central to daily life. Whether it's a beach barbecue, a weekend in the mountains, or watching a local sports match, Australians take full advantage of their sunny climate and stunning natural surroundings. The country is also deeply passionate about sports, with cricket, rugby, Aussie Rules football, and soccer drawing large crowds, while surfing and swimming are part of the national identity.

Australia's economy is robust and modern, with tourism playing a key role. The Australian dollar (AUD) is the official currency, and English is the national language, making it relatively easy for international visitors to communicate and get around. With multiple time zones across the continent, the most common are Australian Eastern Standard Time (AEST) in New South Wales, Victoria, Queensland, and Tasmania, Australian Central Standard Time (ACST) in South Australia and the Northern Territory, and Australian Western Standard Time (AWST) in Western Australia.

In summary, Australia is a destination that offers travelers everything from exciting urban experiences and cultural immersion to incredible natural wonders and wildlife encounters. It is a land of contrasts, where ancient traditions blend with modern life, and where boundless landscapes promise adventure around every corner. As you begin your journey through this remarkable country, expect to be captivated by its beauty, inspired by its rich history, and welcomed by its people. Australia is more than just a place to visit—it's an experience that will stay with you long after you've left its shores.

Chapter 2

Trip Planning Essentials

Planning your trip to Australia involves careful consideration of a variety of factors to ensure a smooth, enjoyable, and unforgettable experience. From understanding the best times to visit to navigating visa requirements, budgeting, and health precautions, a successful Australian adventure starts with thoughtful preparation. Whether you are a seasoned traveler or exploring Australia for the first time, this guide will provide you with all the essentials you need for a stress-free journey.

Best Times to Visit

Australia's sheer size and diversity mean that different regions offer varying climates throughout the year, making it essential to consider when to visit based on your interests and the type of experience you want. Australia's seasons are opposite to those in the Northern Hemisphere. Summer runs from December to February, autumn from March to May, winter from June to August, and spring from September to November.

If you're looking for warm, beach-friendly weather, the summer months are ideal, especially in southern regions like Sydney, Melbourne, and Adelaide. However, summer also brings peak tourist season, meaning crowds and higher prices. If you want to avoid large tourist influxes and secure better deals on flights and accommodations, consider traveling during the shoulder seasons of spring or autumn. These months typically offer pleasant weather and fewer crowds.

The northern part of Australia, including Queensland and the Northern Territory, experiences a tropical climate with wet and dry seasons. The wet season, from November to April, brings heavy rains and can make some areas difficult to access, so plan your visit to these regions during the dry season (May to October) for the best weather and visibility at sites like the Great Barrier Reef.

For those interested in skiing or snow sports, Australia's winter months offer ideal conditions in areas such as the Snowy Mountains and Victoria's Alpine region. Winter is also a great time to visit the Outback as temperatures are cooler and more bearable for exploring national parks and desert landscapes.

Visa and Entry Requirements

Before you travel to Australia, ensure you meet the visa and entry requirements, as these are non-negotiable and strictly enforced. Almost all international travelers need a visa to enter Australia, including tourists, students, and business visitors. The most common visa for short-term tourists is the Electronic Travel Authority (ETA) or the eVisitor visa, both of which can be applied for online. These visas generally allow travelers to stay in Australia for up to 90 days within a 12-month period.

For some travelers, depending on nationality and purpose of visit, additional documentation or visa types may be required. It's always a good idea to check the official Australian Government Department of Home Affairs website for up-to-date visa information and application processes. Processing times vary, so apply for your visa well in advance to avoid any last-minute complications.

You will also need a valid passport with at least six months of validity remaining from the date of your entry into Australia. Keep in mind that even though Australia is a highly developed country, customs and immigration authorities have strict rules about prohibited items, such as certain food products, plants, or animal materials. Be sure to declare any restricted items to avoid penalties.

Budgeting for Your Trip

Australia can be an expensive destination, particularly in its major cities, but with proper budgeting and planning, it is possible to manage costs and still have a rewarding trip. Start by setting a realistic budget that includes accommodation, transportation, meals, and activities. Be aware that while cities like Sydney and Melbourne are known for their high cost of living, more affordable options are available outside urban centers.

Accommodation options range from luxury hotels to budget-friendly hostels, motels, and Airbnb rentals. For those looking to save on lodging, Australia has an extensive network of campsites and caravan parks, many of which are located in scenic national parks or along the coast. If you're traveling with family, consider family-friendly accommodation options like holiday parks that offer cabins, communal kitchens, and recreational activities for children.

Transportation costs vary depending on how you choose to get around. Domestic flights between major cities are convenient but can add up quickly. Consider alternative transport options such as long-distance buses or trains, especially if you have time to explore at a slower pace. Renting a car or campervan is also popular in Australia, offering flexibility and the chance to explore the country's scenic drives and remote areas.

Food costs can also vary widely. Australia is known for its vibrant food scene, with plenty of options from high-end restaurants to affordable street food. For budget-conscious travelers, many supermarkets sell pre-packaged meals, and hostels or Airbnb rentals with kitchens allow you to cook your own meals. Food trucks and local markets are also great for sampling local cuisine without breaking the bank.

Packing for Australia's Varied Climates

Packing for a trip to Australia requires careful consideration of the country's varied climates, as what you need to bring will depend on the regions you plan to visit and the time of year. In general, pack light, breathable clothing for summer trips, especially if you'll be spending time at the beach or in the tropical north. Include essentials like sunscreen, sunglasses, and a wide-brimmed hat to protect yourself from the strong Australian sun.

For winter or visits to the Outback and southern regions, include layers of clothing to adjust to colder temperatures, especially at night. Even in warmer months, some areas experience significant temperature drops after sunset, so a light jacket or sweater is always a good idea.

If you're planning on engaging in outdoor activities like hiking, camping, or visiting national parks, pack sturdy footwear, a water bottle, and protective gear like insect repellent. Some areas, particularly in the Outback, can be isolated with limited access to amenities, so it's a good idea to carry a basic first-aid kit and other essentials like a portable charger.

Traveling with children adds another layer to packing. Be sure to bring enough snacks, entertainment, and comfort items to keep kids happy and occupied during long flights or car rides. Depending on your destination, you may also need specific items like swim gear or hiking boots.

Health Precautions and Travel Insurance

Australia is a safe destination with a well-established healthcare system, but it's still important to take health precautions to ensure a smooth trip. One of the most critical steps is securing travel insurance that covers medical emergencies, trip cancellations, and lost belongings. Healthcare in Australia can be expensive for tourists, so comprehensive travel insurance is a must.

In terms of vaccinations, check with your healthcare provider about any recommended vaccines before your trip. Although there are no mandatory vaccinations for entering Australia, travelers may want to ensure they are up to date on routine immunizations like measles, mumps, rubella (MMR), and tetanus. For those planning to spend time in remote or tropical regions, additional vaccines for diseases such as hepatitis A or typhoid may be advised.

Australia's climate and wildlife also warrant some health precautions. In tropical regions, be mindful of mosquito-borne diseases such as dengue fever and always use insect repellent. If you're visiting the beach, pay attention to safety signs regarding jellyfish or other dangerous marine life. Similarly, if hiking or exploring rural areas, wear appropriate footwear and be aware of snakes and spiders. While encounters are rare, it's best to be prepared.

Family-Specific Tips

Australia is an incredibly family-friendly destination, offering plenty of activities and attractions that appeal to all ages. When planning your trip with children, take into account the family's pace and interests. Don't try to cram too much into a single day—Australia is vast, and rushing from one place to another can leave everyone feeling exhausted. Opt for fewer, more enjoyable activities rather than trying to see it all in one trip.

Many Australian cities offer family-friendly public transport options, and accommodations often cater to families with larger rooms, kitchen facilities, and even babysitting services. Depending on the ages of your children, look for attractions like zoos, aquariums, and theme parks that can provide entertainment and learning experiences for younger travelers.

If traveling with infants or toddlers, it's worth researching baby-friendly amenities in advance. Most major airports have facilities for families with young children, and many restaurants offer high chairs and kids' menus. The Australian lifestyle emphasizes outdoor living, so take advantage of parks, playgrounds, and beaches for some family-friendly fun.

By considering these trip-planning essentials and paying attention to details like timing, budgeting, and health precautions, you're well on your way to an unforgettable Australian adventure. Keep your plans flexible, do your research, and above all, enjoy the experience of exploring one of the most unique and diverse countries in the world.

Chapter 3

Getting Around Australia

Navigating Australia, a vast and diverse country, requires careful planning and an understanding of the various transport options available to suit your itinerary. Whether you are traveling through bustling cities, exploring the coastal regions, or venturing into the remote Outback, Australia's extensive transport network offers multiple ways to get from one destination to another efficiently and comfortably. By choosing the right mode of transport, you can tailor your journey to suit your budget, schedule, and travel preferences while ensuring that you experience the best that this beautiful country has to offer.

Domestic Flights

Given Australia's large landmass, domestic flights are often the most efficient way to cover long distances between major cities and regional destinations. For example, the flight from Sydney to Perth takes about five hours, saving considerable time compared to driving or taking a train. Domestic airlines such as Qantas, Virgin Australia, Jetstar, and Rex connect major cities like Sydney, Melbourne, Brisbane, Perth, and Adelaide with numerous smaller towns and remote regions, offering frequent services throughout the day. These airlines often offer competitive fares, especially if you book in advance or take advantage of low-cost carriers.

For travelers on tighter schedules or those wishing to see as much of Australia as possible within a limited time frame, flying between destinations is highly recommended. However, it's worth noting that domestic flights can add up in cost, especially during peak travel seasons, so it's important to balance your budget and consider alternative transport for shorter distances. Airports in Australia are generally well-connected to public transport systems, making it easy to transfer between your arrival point and your final destination.

Train Travel

Australia offers several iconic train journeys that provide an immersive and scenic way to travel across the country. Train travel in Australia is less about speed and more about the experience, especially for routes like The Ghan, which travels from Adelaide to Darwin, and the Indian Pacific, which connects Sydney and Perth. These long-haul journeys take you through some of Australia's most breathtaking landscapes, from the Outback to coastal plains, and provide a luxurious, relaxed way to cover vast distances. Many of these train journeys offer different levels of service, including sleeper cabins, fine dining, and even guided excursions at certain stops.

For shorter intercity travel, trains are a reliable option, especially in the eastern states where cities are closer together. For instance, the train journey between Sydney and Melbourne takes approximately 11 hours and offers an alternative to flying. Regional trains also connect smaller towns to cities, though services can be limited in frequency. Train travel is generally affordable, but you should book tickets well in advance for long-distance journeys, as these services can fill up quickly, particularly in tourist seasons.

While train travel offers comfort and the chance to take in the scenery, it's not always the fastest way to get around. You may find that trains are better suited to those who enjoy slow travel or want to experience Australia's landscape in a leisurely way.

Road Trips and Self-Drive Options

Australia's vast and varied landscapes make it an ideal destination for road trips, whether you're driving along the stunning coastal highways or venturing deep into the Outback. Renting a car or campervan offers the freedom and flexibility to explore at your own pace, especially in areas where public transport is limited. Self-driving is particularly popular along famous routes such as the Great Ocean Road in Victoria, which offers jaw-dropping coastal views, or the Pacific Coast Highway, which stretches from Sydney to Brisbane. These routes allow you to stop at picturesque towns, national parks, and beaches along the way, making the journey itself as enjoyable as the destinations.

Driving in Australia is relatively easy for international visitors, particularly those from countries that drive on the left-hand side of the road. Major car rental companies operate in all major cities and airports, offering a range of vehicles from economy cars to 4WDs and campervans. It's important to note that driving in Australia's cities differs from driving in rural or remote areas. In cities like Sydney, Melbourne, or Brisbane, traffic can be heavy, parking can be expensive, and many roads require toll payments. Using a GPS or navigation app will help you navigate efficiently and avoid unexpected fees.

For those planning to explore the Outback or remote regions, a 4WD vehicle is highly recommended, as roads can be unpaved or difficult to navigate in standard vehicles. Make sure you are well-prepared with enough water, fuel, and emergency supplies, as remote areas often lack services and amenities. Mobile phone coverage can also be limited in these regions, so having a satellite phone or personal locator beacon (PLB) may provide added safety. It's also a good idea to familiarize yourself with driving conditions in the

Outback, as distances between towns can be long, wildlife can be a hazard on roads, and weather conditions may change rapidly.

Public Transport in Cities

Australia's major cities have efficient public transport systems that make it easy to get around without the need for a car. Sydney, Melbourne, Brisbane, Adelaide, and Perth all have extensive networks of buses, trains, and trams that connect city centers with outer suburbs and popular tourist attractions. In Sydney, the Opal card provides access to buses, trains, ferries, and light rail, while in Melbourne, the Myki card offers travel across the city's iconic trams, trains, and buses. These smartcards can be topped up online or at stations and are essential for easy travel around the city.

Melbourne's tram system, in particular, is a highlight for travelers, as it is the largest urban tram network in the world and provides a scenic and convenient way to explore the city. Sydney's ferries offer another unique way to get around, with routes that provide stunning views of Sydney Harbour, the Opera House, and the Harbour

Bridge. Public transport is generally affordable, with capped daily fares in many cities, making it a cost-effective way to explore urban areas.

However, public transport services can vary in frequency and coverage, especially in outer suburbs or smaller towns, where it may be less reliable. While public transport is great for city travel, if you plan to explore more remote or rural areas, renting a car may be more practical.

Eco-Friendly Transport Options

Australia is increasingly focused on sustainability, and eco-conscious travelers will find a growing number of green transport options. Biking is a popular and eco-friendly way to explore cities, especially in places like Melbourne, where bike lanes are extensive, and bike-sharing schemes like Melbourne Bike Share are widely available. Many other cities, including Brisbane and Canberra, also have bike-sharing programs that make it easy to rent bikes for short-term use. Biking allows you to enjoy the outdoors while minimizing your carbon footprint.

Walking is another excellent way to get around cities, especially if you're exploring compact areas like Sydney's Circular Quay or Melbourne's central business district. Most Australian cities are highly walkable, with pedestrian-friendly areas, parks, and scenic paths that allow you to discover urban environments at a relaxed pace. In coastal cities, walking trails along the beaches provide breathtaking views and access to quieter spots away from the city bustle.

For longer trips, travelers can choose eco-friendly transport options like electric car rentals or public buses that run on cleaner energy sources. In recent years, some Australian tour companies have also begun offering carbon-neutral tours that focus on sustainable practices and reducing environmental impact.

Ride-Sharing and Taxis

Ride-sharing services like Uber and Ola operate widely in Australia's major cities and offer a convenient alternative to taxis for getting around urban areas. These services are often cheaper than traditional taxis and allow travelers to book rides through mobile apps, providing flexibility and ease of payment. In addition to ride-sharing, taxis are available throughout most cities and towns, though they can be more expensive, particularly late at night or during peak times.

Ride-sharing services are a good option for travelers who prefer door-to-door transport without the hassle of renting a car or navigating public transport. For airport transfers or trips between hotels and attractions, ride-sharing can save time and effort, especially if you're traveling with luggage. However, in more remote areas, these services may be unavailable, so it's essential to plan accordingly.

Choosing the Right Transport for Your Itinerary

The transport you choose in Australia should align with your itinerary and travel style. For those focusing on urban exploration, public transport, biking, and walking are ideal for getting around efficiently while experiencing the local culture. If you're planning a road trip or exploring remote regions, renting a car or campervan will give you the freedom to travel at your own pace and access places that public transport can't reach.

If you're short on time but want to cover as much ground as possible, domestic flights provide a fast and convenient way to connect between cities and regions. For a slower, more scenic journey, consider taking the train for a more relaxed and immersive travel experience.

Ultimately, getting around Australia involves a mix of options, and many travelers find that combining different modes of transport allows them to make the most of their time and see a wider variety of places. The key is to research your options, plan ahead, and be flexible, so you can tailor your transport choices to your own unique adventure.

Navigating Australia is part of the adventure itself. By choosing the right transport for your itinerary, you'll enhance your experience of this diverse and beautiful country, ensuring that every journey, whether by air, road, or rail, is as enjoyable as the destination.

Chapter 4

Iconic Australia: Must-See Destinations

Australia is a land of immense beauty and diversity, offering a captivating array of must-see destinations that appeal to every kind of traveler. From vibrant cities brimming with culture to breathtaking natural wonders that have captured the world's imagination, Australia is a country that surprises and delights at every turn. Whether you're drawn to the pulsating energy of the cities or the tranquil allure of the wilderness, this vast continent has something to offer. In this chapter, we will explore Australia's most iconic destinations, offering insider tips on the best attractions, experiences, and hidden gems that will make your journey unforgettable.

Sydney: The Heart of Australia's Coast

Sydney is often the first city that comes to mind when thinking of Australia, and for good reason. Its stunning harbor, famous landmarks, and vibrant culture make it a must-visit destination for travelers. The jewel in Sydney's crown is undoubtedly the Sydney Opera House, an architectural marvel that stands proudly on the waterfront, offering breathtaking views of Sydney Harbour. A visit to the Opera House, whether for a tour, a performance, or simply to admire its beauty, is an essential part of any trip to Sydney.

Just a stone's throw away is the Sydney Harbour Bridge, an iconic structure that can be appreciated from afar or, for the adventurous, up close through the exhilarating BridgeClimb experience. This guided ascent to the top of the bridge offers panoramic views of the city and is a thrilling way to see Sydney from above. Circular Quay, located near these landmarks, is the perfect starting point for ferry rides to other key spots like Manly Beach and Taronga Zoo.

Bondi Beach, another iconic attraction, is synonymous with Sydney's laid-back, beach-loving lifestyle. Whether you want to swim, surf, or simply soak up the sun, Bondi offers a quintessential Australian beach experience. For a more secluded spot, the Bondi to Coogee coastal walk offers spectacular views and access to lesser-known beaches along the way. Sydney's thriving food and arts scenes are also worth exploring, with neighborhoods like Surry Hills and Newtown offering cutting-edge dining and creative experiences that reflect the city's cosmopolitan nature.

Melbourne: A Cultural and Artistic Hub

In contrast to Sydney's coastal allure, Melbourne offers a more bohemian vibe, often referred to as the cultural capital of Australia. Known for its art galleries, theaters, and coffee culture, Melbourne is a city where creativity thrives. The city's laneways are a treasure trove of hidden gems, from street art to boutique cafes and shops. A walk through the laneways, particularly Hosier Lane, will reveal some of the best street art in the world, making Melbourne a haven for art lovers.

The iconic Federation Square is a hub of cultural activity, with its distinctive architecture and museums like the National Gallery of Victoria and the Australian Centre for the Moving Image. Melbourne's coffee culture is legendary, and a visit to one of the many specialty coffee shops is a must for caffeine lovers. The city is also home to a diverse culinary scene, with its many restaurants reflecting the multicultural makeup of the city. From high-end dining to food trucks and everything in between, Melbourne is a foodie's paradise.

For sports enthusiasts, Melbourne is the place to be. It hosts major events such as the Australian Open and the Melbourne Cup, and its passionate sports culture can be experienced firsthand by attending a game of Aussie rules football at the Melbourne Cricket Ground. Melbourne is also the gateway to the Great Ocean Road, one of Australia's most scenic drives. The road winds along the coastline, passing through charming towns and offering awe-inspiring views of landmarks like the Twelve Apostles, limestone stacks that rise dramatically from the ocean. This road trip is an unforgettable experience, showcasing the natural beauty of the region.

The Great Barrier Reef: A Natural Wonder

The Great Barrier Reef is one of Australia's most iconic and awe-inspiring destinations, drawing visitors from around the globe to witness its stunning marine biodiversity. Stretching over 2,300 kilometers along the Queensland coast, it is the largest coral reef system in the world and a UNESCO World Heritage site. Whether you're a seasoned diver or a first-time snorkeler, exploring the vibrant underwater world of the Great Barrier Reef is an unforgettable experience.

Cairns and Port Douglas serve as popular gateways to the reef, offering numerous tour options for exploring this natural wonder. Snorkeling and diving trips provide the chance to see an incredible array of marine life, from colorful coral formations to tropical fish, turtles, and even sharks. For those who prefer to stay dry, glass-bottom boat tours and semi-submersible vessels offer a unique way to view the reef without getting wet.

Beyond the reef itself, the surrounding islands, such as the Whitsundays and Lady Elliot Island, offer beautiful beaches and luxury resorts. A visit to these islands allows for a more relaxed experience of the reef, with opportunities to hike, swim, and unwind in paradise-like settings. The Great Barrier Reef is also an important destination for eco-conscious travelers, as many tour operators now focus on sustainability and reef preservation efforts, ensuring that this natural wonder can be enjoyed by future generations.

Uluru: The Spiritual Heart of Australia

Deep in the heart of the Australian Outback lies Uluru, one of the country's most sacred and iconic landmarks. This massive sandstone monolith rises 348 meters from the desert floor and is revered by the indigenous Anangu people, who have lived in the area for thousands of years. A visit to Uluru is not only a chance to witness its breathtaking beauty but also to connect with the deep spiritual significance it holds for the local Aboriginal culture.

One of the most magical experiences at Uluru is watching the sunrise or sunset as the colors of the rock change dramatically in the shifting light. These moments are truly unforgettable, as the rock seems to glow in hues of red, orange, and purple. Visitors can explore the base of Uluru by foot, learning about its cultural and geological significance through guided walks or self-guided tours. The nearby Kata Tjuta (The Olgas), a series of large rock formations, is another must-see attraction in the area, offering stunning landscapes and hiking opportunities.

While Uluru itself is a powerful symbol of Australia's natural and cultural heritage, the surrounding region, including the town of Alice Springs, provides further insight into Outback life. Camel rides, Aboriginal cultural experiences, and visits to ancient rock art sites are just a few of the ways to deepen your connection to this remarkable region.

The Outback: Exploring Australia's Vast Wilderness

The Australian Outback is a vast and remote region that embodies the rugged spirit of the country. Stretching across much of the continent, the Outback is characterized by red desert sands, endless horizons, and a sense of isolation that is both daunting and awe-inspiring. For those seeking adventure and a deeper understanding of

Australia's natural environment, a journey into the Outback is an essential part of any trip.

Driving through the Outback offers a unique experience, where you can witness Australia's unique wildlife, such as kangaroos, emus, and even wild camels. The remote towns and roadhouses scattered throughout the Outback provide a glimpse into the lives of those who call this region home. Towns like Coober Pedy, famous for its opal mines and underground homes, offer a quirky and fascinating stop on your Outback journey.

The Outback is also home to some of Australia's most significant national parks, such as Kakadu National Park in the Northern Territory and Karijini National Park in Western Australia. These parks are teeming with unique wildlife, stunning waterfalls, and ancient rock art sites that offer a glimpse into the rich Aboriginal history of the region. Exploring the Outback requires preparation and respect for the environment, as the remote conditions can be challenging, but the rewards are immense for those willing to venture off the beaten path.

Brisbane: A Gateway to the Sunshine and Gold Coasts

Brisbane, the capital of Queensland, is a vibrant city that serves as a gateway to two of Australia's most famous coastal regions: the Sunshine Coast to the north and the Gold Coast to the south. Brisbane itself is a lively city with a subtropical climate, offering a blend of urban sophistication and laid-back charm. The city's South Bank precinct is a cultural hub, home to the Queensland Art Gallery, the Gallery of Modern Art, and the Queensland Museum. The parklands along the Brisbane River provide a beautiful setting for outdoor activities, from cycling to picnicking.

Brisbane's proximity to the Sunshine and Gold Coasts makes it an ideal base for exploring these famous beach destinations. The Sunshine Coast is known for its relaxed atmosphere, beautiful beaches, and charming towns like Noosa, which is famous for its surf breaks and national park. The Gold Coast, on the other hand, is known for its glitzy skyline, theme parks, and vibrant nightlife. Both regions offer excellent opportunities for surfing, swimming, and exploring Queensland's natural beauty.

Whether you're seeking adventure in the form of water sports and hiking or prefer to relax on pristine beaches, Brisbane and its surrounding coasts provide a perfect balance of city and coastal experiences.

Perth: A Western Australian Gem

On the opposite side of the continent lies Perth, the capital of Western Australia and one of the most isolated cities in the world. Despite its remote location, Perth offers a dynamic mix of outdoor adventure, cultural experiences, and laid-back living. The city's location along the Swan River and its proximity to the Indian Ocean make it a haven for water activities, from sailing to snorkeling.

Kings Park, one of the largest inner-city parks in the world, offers stunning views of the city skyline and the river, as well as beautiful botanical gardens and walking trails. Fremantle, located just outside Perth, is a historic port city known for its vibrant arts

Australia is a land of contrasts, offering everything from bustling cities to remote deserts, pristine beaches to lush rainforests. The sheer variety of experiences available to travelers is what makes it such an exciting and memorable destination. Whether you're drawn to the vibrant cultural scenes of Sydney and Melbourne, the natural wonders of the Great Barrier Reef and Uluru, or the rugged beauty of the Outback, each region of Australia offers something unique and unforgettable.

As you embark on your journey through these iconic destinations, embrace the diversity that Australia has to offer. Take time to explore beyond the tourist hotspots and discover the hidden gems that give each place its distinct character. Engage with the local culture, whether it's through sampling regional cuisine, learning about Aboriginal heritage, or simply connecting with the friendly locals.

No matter where your travels take you in Australia, you're sure to be captivated by the rich tapestry of landscapes, cultures, and experiences that define this extraordinary country. Let the magic of Australia inspire you to explore deeply, enjoy fully, and create memories that will last a lifetime.

Chapter 5

Hidden Gems of Australia

Australia is known for its iconic landmarks, but it's the hidden gems tucked away from the beaten path that often leave the most lasting impressions. These lesser-known destinations showcase the raw beauty of the land, offering serene escapes from the hustle and bustle of popular tourist spots. Whether you're searching for tranquil national parks, remote islands, or charming small towns that breathe authenticity, this chapter will inspire you to venture off the typical tourist route and uncover the soul of Australia. Here, nature remains untouched, wildlife thrives, and adventure waits for those willing to explore further.

Unspoiled National Parks and Wilderness Escapes

Australia's national parks are some of the most beautiful and diverse in the world, yet many remain relatively undiscovered by tourists. Beyond the well-known parks like Kakadu and the Blue Mountains, there are countless smaller sanctuaries offering unique landscapes and wildlife encounters. One such gem is Booderee National Park, located on the southern coast of New South Wales. It's a secluded paradise where crystal-clear waters meet powdery white sand beaches, all set within a lush natural environment. Whether you're swimming in the pristine waters of Green Patch Beach, camping under a blanket of stars, or exploring the Botanic Gardens, Booderee provides a perfect escape for those seeking solitude and natural beauty.

Further north, Nitmiluk National Park in the Northern Territory offers a dramatic and peaceful landscape of gorges, rivers, and rock formations. The park is home to the Katherine Gorge, a series of 13 stunning gorges carved through ancient sandstone. Visitors can canoe along the river, hike scenic trails, or take a cultural tour led by the local Jawoyn people, who share the significance of the land and their connection to it. With its untouched beauty and rich cultural heritage, Nitmiluk is an ideal destination for those looking to connect with nature in a meaningful way.

In Tasmania, Mount Field National Park offers a hidden oasis of waterfalls, alpine landscapes, and ancient rainforest. A visit to Russell Falls, one of Tasmania's most beautiful waterfalls, is a must, and the surrounding trails provide opportunities to spot wildlife like platypuses, echidnas, and wombats. The park's combination of diverse landscapes and peaceful surroundings makes it an unforgettable destination for nature lovers.

Remote Islands Offering Seclusion and Adventure

Australia's islands are often synonymous with tropical paradises like the Whitsundays, but beyond these popular destinations lie islands that offer true seclusion and adventure. Lord Howe Island, located off the coast of New South Wales, is a UNESCO World Heritage site that remains one of Australia's most preserved and tranquil destinations. With only a limited number of visitors allowed on the island at any time, Lord Howe feels like a private paradise. Here, you can snorkel in pristine lagoons, hike through lush forests, and observe abundant birdlife, all without the crowds. It's an idyllic retreat for those seeking unspoiled natural beauty and a slower pace of life.

Kangaroo Island, located off the coast of South Australia, is another hidden gem that offers a perfect blend of wildlife, natural beauty, and rugged coastline. The island is a haven for wildlife enthusiasts, with opportunities to see kangaroos, koalas, sea lions, and penguins in their natural habitats. The island's beaches are some of the most beautiful and untouched in the country, such as Vivonne Bay and Stokes Bay, where you can enjoy pristine sands and clear waters away from the tourist crowds. Kangaroo Island also boasts unique geological formations, like the Remarkable Rocks and Admirals Arch, which are must-sees for any visitor.

For a more tropical escape, Fitzroy Island off the coast of Cairns in Queensland offers a hidden paradise of coral reefs, rainforest, and secluded beaches. The island is home to the Turtle Rehabilitation Centre, where visitors can learn about the conservation of sea turtles and see the efforts being made to protect these endangered animals. Whether you're snorkeling on the Great Barrier Reef, hiking through the rainforest, or simply relaxing on the beach, Fitzroy Island provides a serene and environmentally conscious escape.

Charming Small Towns and Authentic Local Experiences

Australia's charm isn't limited to its cities and coastal resorts. The country is home to countless small towns, each offering its own unique character and a chance to experience authentic Australian life. One such town is Yamba, located on the northern coast of New South Wales. Known for its beautiful beaches and relaxed atmosphere, Yamba has been quietly gaining a reputation as one of Australia's best coastal towns. It's a place where you can surf uncrowded waves, enjoy fresh seafood, and experience a slower, more authentic pace of life. The nearby Angourie Point is renowned among surfers as one of the best surf breaks in the country, while the town itself offers a warm and welcoming community.

In Victoria, the town of Bright in the alpine region offers a completely different kind of charm. Surrounded by mountains, rivers, and forests, Bright is a hub for outdoor activities such as hiking, cycling, and kayaking. The town comes alive in autumn when the trees turn brilliant shades of red, orange, and yellow, creating a picturesque landscape that feels like something out of a storybook. With its charming cafes, boutique shops, and proximity to Mount Buffalo National Park, Bright is a perfect destination for those seeking a blend of adventure and relaxation in a small-town setting.

For those interested in Australia's gold rush history, the town of Beechworth in Victoria is a hidden gem that has preserved its heritage with pride. The town's well-preserved architecture, historic sites, and museums offer a fascinating glimpse into Australia's colonial past. Visitors can explore the Beechworth Historic Courthouse, take a walk through the gold rush-era cemetery, or simply enjoy the town's boutique wineries and restaurants. Beechworth is also known for its natural beauty, with nearby waterfalls and walking trails offering a peaceful escape into nature.

Wildlife Sanctuaries and Secluded Beaches

Australia is renowned for its unique wildlife, and while popular zoos and animal parks draw crowds, the country is also home to hidden wildlife sanctuaries that offer more intimate and authentic experiences. Bonorong Wildlife Sanctuary in Tasmania is one such place, where visitors can get up close and personal with rescued and rehabilitated animals, including Tasmanian devils, wombats, and quolls. The sanctuary's focus on conservation and education provides an enriching experience for visitors who want to learn more about Australia's native species and the efforts being made to protect them.

For beach lovers, Australia is a paradise of secluded stretches of sand that remain blissfully free of crowds. The Sapphire Coast in New South Wales is one such destination, offering stunning beaches like Tathra and Pambula that are perfect for swimming, surfing, or simply relaxing in peace. The region's unspoiled coastline, coupled with its clear waters and abundant marine life, makes it an ideal spot for those seeking tranquility and natural beauty.

In Western Australia, the beaches of Esperance are some of the most beautiful and untouched in the country. The region's white sand and turquoise waters create a postcard-perfect scene, with highlights including Lucky Bay, known for its resident kangaroos that laze on the beach, and Twilight Beach, which is often voted one of the best beaches in Australia. These secluded beaches offer the kind of peaceful escape that many travelers dream of, far removed from the crowds and commercialization of more popular tourist destinations.

Scenic Road Trips to Uncover Australia's True Beauty

One of the best ways to uncover Australia's hidden gems is by hitting the open road and embarking on a scenic road trip. While the Great Ocean Road is famous worldwide, there are countless other routes that offer equally spectacular views and more secluded experiences. The Savannah Way, which stretches from Cairns in Queensland to Broome in Western Australia, takes travelers through remote Outback towns, lush wetlands, and rugged escarpments. Along the way, you'll discover hidden waterfalls, Aboriginal rock art sites, and vast stretches of untouched wilderness that few tourists ever see.

In South Australia, the Eyre Peninsula offers a road trip filled with breathtaking coastal scenery, wildlife encounters, and small-town charm. The drive takes you along the rugged coastline, where you can spot sea lions, dolphins, and even great white sharks. The region's seafood is some of the best in the country, and a visit to the town of Coffin Bay to sample its famous oysters is a must for any foodie. The Eyre Peninsula's combination of natural beauty, wildlife, and delicious local produce makes it an ideal destination for those looking to explore Australia's hidden treasures by car.

Western Australia's Coral Coast is another hidden gem of a road trip, offering stunning coastal views, pristine beaches, and access to lesser-known natural wonders like the Pinnacles Desert and Kalbarri National Park. The drive from Perth to Exmouth takes you through remote coastal towns, past striking cliffs, and offers opportunities to snorkel with whale sharks at Ningaloo Reef. It's a journey filled with adventure and tranquility, showcasing the best of Western Australia's natural beauty.

Finally, Australia's hidden gems are the places that reveal the true heart of this diverse and captivating country. Whether it's a remote national park, a charming small town, or a secluded beach, these lesser-known destinations offer authentic experiences that go beyond the typical tourist itinerary. By venturing off the beaten path, you'll uncover the soul of Australia—a place where nature remains untouched, wildlife roams free, and the pace of life slows down to allow you to truly connect with the land and its people.

These hidden gems offer more than just beautiful scenery; they provide a deeper understanding of Australia's cultural heritage, wildlife, and way of life. For travelers seeking adventure, tranquility, or simply a different perspective on this vast country, Australia's best-kept secrets are waiting to be discovered. Let this chapter be your guide to finding those places that will make your journey uniquely memorable

Chapter 6

Adventure and Nature in Australia

Australia is an adventurer's playground, a land where thrilling experiences and awe-inspiring natural beauty intertwine to create memories that last a lifetime. Whether you are drawn to the vibrant marine life of the Great Barrier Reef, the vast, rugged landscapes of the Outback, or the dense, mysterious rainforests, Australia offers endless opportunities to connect with nature. This chapter is a guide to some of the most exhilarating outdoor activities and nature experiences the country has to offer, encouraging you to embrace the wild side of Australia while also being mindful of its environmental treasures.

Exploring the Great Barrier Reef: A Marine Paradise

The Great Barrier Reef is one of Australia's most celebrated natural wonders and a bucket-list destination for nature lovers and adventure seekers alike. Stretching over 2,300 kilometers along the Queensland coast, the reef is the world's largest coral system and home to an incredible array of marine life. Whether you're an experienced diver or a first-time snorkeler, the Great Barrier Reef offers a unique opportunity to witness the underwater world in all its vibrant glory.

Snorkeling and diving in the reef's crystal-clear waters provide unforgettable encounters with brightly colored coral gardens, schools of tropical fish, sea turtles, and even larger species like manta rays and reef sharks. There are various access points along the coast, with popular departure towns including Cairns, Port Douglas, and Airlie Beach, where eco-certified tours ensure that visitors can explore the reef sustainably. The Outer Reef, less frequented by tourists, offers some of the most pristine dive sites, allowing for a more intimate experience with Australia's marine paradise.

Beyond diving and snorkeling, the reef also offers opportunities for glass-bottom boat tours, underwater observatories, and even scenic flights for those who prefer to witness the beauty of the reef from above. No matter how you choose to explore, the Great Barrier Reef provides an awe-inspiring connection to nature's underwater marvels.

Hiking Through Australia's Diverse Landscapes

Australia's diverse landscapes offer a wide range of hiking experiences, from tropical rainforests to arid desert trails, alpine regions to rugged coastal paths. No matter your level of experience, there's a trail in Australia to suit every adventurer. One of the most iconic hiking experiences in Australia is the Larapinta Trail in the Northern Territory. This 223-kilometer trail traverses the stunning West MacDonnell Ranges, offering breathtaking views of ancient mountain ranges, deep gorges, and expansive plains. The trail can be tackled in sections or as a multi-day adventure, allowing hikers to immerse themselves in the Outback's raw beauty while encountering rare wildlife and Aboriginal cultural sites along the way.

In contrast to the arid Outback, Tasmania offers lush, temperate rainforests and alpine landscapes for hikers to explore. The Overland Track, a world-renowned 65-kilometer trail in Tasmania's Cradle Mountain-Lake St. Clair National Park, takes hikers through pristine wilderness areas filled with waterfalls, alpine lakes, and ancient forests. This trail is ideal for those seeking both adventure and tranquility, as the remote setting allows for moments of peaceful reflection amidst the stunning scenery.

For coastal lovers, the Great Ocean Walk in Victoria offers a spectacular journey along Australia's southern coastline. Stretching over 100 kilometers, this trail passes through diverse landscapes of eucalyptus forests, sandy beaches, and dramatic cliffs, all while providing sweeping views of the Southern Ocean. As you hike, you may encounter koalas lounging in trees, kangaroos grazing in open fields, and a myriad of birdlife that call this coastal region home. The trail also takes you to the famous Twelve Apostles, a collection of limestone stacks that rise majestically from the ocean, creating a sight that's sure to leave a lasting impression.

The Outback: A Journey Into the Heart of Australia

The Australian Outback is a vast, untamed wilderness that offers a true sense of adventure and isolation. It's a place where the land stretches endlessly towards the horizon, the skies are impossibly wide, and the silence is profound. Exploring the Outback allows travelers to connect with the raw beauty of the landscape, from the red deserts of the Northern Territory to the ancient rock formations of Western Australia.

One of the most iconic Outback experiences is a visit to Uluru, the massive sandstone monolith that rises dramatically from the red desert in the heart of the country. Watching the sunrise or sunset over Uluru is a transformative experience, as the colors of the rock shift and change with the light, creating a surreal and almost spiritual atmosphere. Nearby, Kata Tjuta (the Olgas) offers a less-visited but equally awe-inspiring natural wonder, with its series of large, dome-shaped rock formations providing fantastic opportunities for hiking and exploration.

Further west, the Kimberley region in Western Australia offers an Outback experience like no other, with its rugged gorges, remote waterfalls, and rich Aboriginal history. The Gibb River Road is one of Australia's great adventure drives, taking travelers through the heart of the Kimberley and offering access to hidden gems like El Questro Gorge, Bell Gorge, and the stunning Mitchell Falls. It's a journey that requires preparation and a sense of adventure, but for those willing to venture into this remote corner of the country, the rewards are spectacular.

Wildlife Encounters: From Rainforests to Deserts

Australia is a land teeming with wildlife, and encountering animals in their natural habitats is one of the country's most rewarding experiences. From kangaroos hopping across open plains to koalas napping in eucalyptus trees, the opportunity to observe Australia's unique wildlife is a highlight for many travelers. In the tropical rainforests of Queensland's Daintree National Park, visitors can spot rare and endangered species like the cassowary, a large flightless bird that roams the forest floor. Guided wildlife tours provide an opportunity to learn about the region's rich biodiversity while ensuring that interactions with animals are done respectfully and sustainably.

For those seeking marine wildlife encounters, Ningaloo Reef in Western Australia offers the chance to swim with whale sharks, the gentle giants of the ocean. This once-in-a-lifetime experience allows you to snorkel alongside these majestic creatures as they glide through the turquoise waters of the Indian Ocean. The reef is also home to manta rays, dolphins, and humpback whales, making it a must-visit destination for marine enthusiasts.

Kangaroo Island, off the coast of South Australia, is a wildlife haven where visitors can see sea lions basking on the beaches, koalas lounging in trees, and kangaroos grazing in open fields. The island's conservation areas, such as Flinders Chase National Park, offer opportunities to see these animals in their natural habitats while also contributing to the protection of the region's unique ecosystems.

Extreme Sports: Skydiving, Surfing, and Beyond

For adrenaline junkies, Australia offers a wealth of extreme sports and adventure activities that will get your heart racing. Skydiving is one of the most popular extreme sports in Australia, with locations such as Mission Beach in Queensland and Wollongong in New South Wales offering the chance to leap from a plane and freefall towards stunning coastal landscapes before your parachute opens, allowing you to float gently back to earth.

Australia's beaches are also world-famous for their surfing conditions, with spots like Bells Beach in Victoria and Snapper Rocks on the Gold Coast attracting surfers from around the world. Whether you're an experienced surfer or a beginner looking to catch your first wave, Australia's diverse coastline offers something for everyone. Surf schools along the coast provide lessons for those new to the sport, while experienced surfers can take on the challenge of riding the powerful waves at some of the country's more famous breaks.

Beyond skydiving and surfing, Australia offers a range of other extreme sports, from bungee jumping in Cairns to white-water rafting on the Tully River. No matter what kind of thrill you're seeking, Australia's diverse landscapes and outdoor culture provide endless opportunities for adventure.

Eco-Tourism: Exploring Nature Sustainably

As travelers become increasingly aware of the importance of sustainable tourism, Australia offers a variety of eco-tourism experiences that allow you to explore the country's natural beauty while minimizing your impact on the environment. Many national parks and wildlife sanctuaries in Australia prioritize conservation and education, offering guided tours that provide insight into the delicate ecosystems that make the country so unique.

For example, the Maria Island Walk in Tasmania is an award-winning eco-tourism experience that takes visitors through pristine wilderness areas while minimizing their environmental footprint. The walk is led by knowledgeable guides who provide insight into the region's flora, fauna, and history, and the tour's accommodation options are designed to have minimal impact on the surrounding environment.

In Queensland, the Daintree Rainforest is a UNESCO World Heritage site that offers a range of eco-friendly tours, from guided walks with Aboriginal guides to river cruises that allow you to spot wildlife like crocodiles and tree kangaroos. These experiences not only offer a deeper connection to nature but also contribute to the preservation of Australia's natural wonders for future generations to enjoy.

Embracing Adventure and Nature in Australia

Australia is a country that invites you to step outside your comfort zone and embrace the natural world in all its glory. Whether you're diving into the vibrant waters of the Great Barrier Reef, hiking through remote wilderness areas, or embarking on an Outback adventure, Australia's landscapes provide endless opportunities for adventure and connection with nature. By exploring responsibly and sustainably, you'll not only create unforgettable memories but also contribute to the preservation of the very ecosystems that make Australia so special.

Chapter 7

Australian Food and Drink

Australia's food and drink culture is as diverse and dynamic as the country itself, shaped by its indigenous heritage, colonial history, and multicultural influences. From traditional favorites like Vegemite and meat pies to world-class wines and innovative fine dining, Australia offers a gastronomic journey that caters to all tastes and preferences. This chapter will delve into the rich and varied culinary landscape of Australia, highlighting must-try dishes, top wine regions, and unique dining experiences that make the country a paradise for food and drink lovers. Whether you're indulging in gourmet cuisine, savoring local wines, or seeking vegetarian and gluten-free options, Australia's food scene promises to be a feast for the senses.

Traditional Dishes: A Taste of Australia

When it comes to traditional Australian dishes, several iconic foods immediately come to mind, offering a true taste of the country's heritage and culture. Vegemite, perhaps the most famous (or infamous) of Australian foods, is a thick, salty spread made from leftover brewer's yeast extract. For many Australians, spreading Vegemite on toast is a breakfast staple, and while it may not appeal to everyone's palate, trying it is almost a rite of passage for visitors to the country.

Meat pies are another beloved Australian classic. Often referred to as the nation's unofficial dish, these handheld savory pies are filled with minced meat, gravy, and sometimes vegetables, all encased in a flaky pastry shell. Found in bakeries, cafes, and even at sports events, the meat pie is a quintessential Aussie comfort food that reflects the country's British colonial influence.

Pavlova, on the other hand, is Australia's most famous dessert and is often served at special occasions, particularly during the holiday season. Named after the Russian ballerina Anna Pavlova, this meringue-based dessert is light and fluffy on the inside, with a crisp exterior, typically topped with whipped cream and fresh fruit like strawberries, passionfruit, or kiwi. While New Zealand also claims pavlova as its own, it remains a cherished part of Australian cuisine.

For those seeking a more adventurous culinary experience, the traditional foods of Australia's Aboriginal people, often referred to as "bush tucker," offer a unique insight into the country's indigenous food culture. Bush tucker includes ingredients such as kangaroo, emu, and crocodile, as well as native fruits, seeds, and herbs like wattleseed and finger lime. These ingredients are increasingly being incorporated into modern Australian cuisine, with many chefs embracing the flavors and techniques of Aboriginal cooking to create innovative and delicious dishes.

Wine and Beer: A Journey Through Australia's Top Regions

Australia is renowned for its world-class wines, with several regions across the country producing award-winning varietals that have gained international acclaim. Whether you're a wine connoisseur or a casual enthusiast, a visit to one of

Australia's many wine regions is a must for any food and drink lover.

The Barossa Valley in South Australia is perhaps the most famous of Australia's wine regions, known for its robust Shiraz and full-bodied red wines. The region is home to some of the country's oldest vineyards, with many wineries offering cellar door tastings, vineyard tours, and gourmet food experiences. Visitors can sample a wide range of wines, from rich reds to crisp whites, while also enjoying the picturesque landscapes of rolling vineyards and charming country towns.

Margaret River, located in Western Australia, is another top wine region that has gained a reputation for producing exceptional wines, particularly Chardonnay and Cabernet Sauvignon. In addition to its wineries, Margaret River is also known for its craft breweries, making it an ideal destination for both wine and beer lovers. Many of the region's wineries and breweries also feature gourmet restaurants that highlight local produce, offering visitors a chance to indulge in food and drink pairings that showcase the best of the region.

Hunter Valley, located just a short drive from Sydney, is one of Australia's oldest wine regions and is famous for its Semillon and Shiraz. The region offers a mix of boutique wineries and larger, more established producers, with many offering wine tastings, vineyard tours, and even hot air balloon rides over the vineyards. For those who prefer sparkling wines, Tasmania is the place to visit, with its cool climate providing ideal conditions for producing high-quality sparkling varietals.

In addition to its wines, Australia has a thriving craft beer scene, with microbreweries and brewpubs popping up across the country. The states of Victoria and Western Australia, in particular, are known for their craft beer cultures, with breweries experimenting with unique flavors and techniques to create innovative beers that reflect the local landscape. Many breweries also offer food menus that complement their beers, making them a great option for a casual dining experience.

Local Dining: From Fine Dining to Food Trucks

Australia's dining scene is as diverse as its population, with influences from around the world shaping the country's culinary landscape. From fine dining establishments to bustling food markets and food trucks, Australia offers a wide range of dining experiences to suit every taste and budget.

In recent years, Australia has gained international recognition for its fine dining scene, with several restaurants earning prestigious awards and Michelin stars. Sydney and Melbourne, in particular, are home to some of the country's most acclaimed restaurants, where chefs combine modern techniques with fresh, local ingredients to create innovative and exciting dishes. Restaurants like Quay in Sydney and Attica in Melbourne offer multi-course tasting menus that take diners on a culinary journey through Australia's unique flavors and ingredients.

For those seeking a more casual dining experience, Australia's food truck scene has exploded in popularity in recent years, offering a wide range of cuisines from around the world. From Mexican tacos to Japanese sushi, Italian pizza to Middle Eastern falafel, food trucks can be found in cities and towns across the country, often gathering in designated food truck parks or at special events. These mobile eateries offer an affordable and delicious way to sample different cuisines while also supporting local, independent food businesses.

Australia is also home to a vibrant cafe culture, with cities like Melbourne and Sydney boasting some of the best coffee in the world. In addition to serving up expertly crafted flat whites and cappuccinos, many cafes also offer a range of breakfast and brunch options, from smashed avocado on toast to acai bowls and poached eggs with smoked salmon. Australia's cafes are known for their emphasis on fresh, local ingredients and creative, healthy dishes that cater to a range of dietary preferences.

Culinary Diversity: Vegetarian, Vegan, and Gluten-Free Options

Australia's food scene has evolved to cater to a wide range of dietary needs, with many restaurants and cafes offering vegetarian, vegan, and gluten-free options. As more people adopt plant-based diets and seek out healthier, more sustainable food choices, Australia's culinary landscape has embraced this trend, offering a variety of delicious and innovative dishes that cater to all preferences.

In cities like Melbourne and Sydney, vegetarian and vegan restaurants have become increasingly popular, offering creative and flavorful plant-based dishes that go beyond the standard salads and veggie burgers. Many of these restaurants focus on using locally sourced, organic ingredients, with menus that change seasonally to reflect what's fresh and in-season. Even non-vegetarian restaurants often feature extensive vegetarian and vegan options, ensuring that everyone can enjoy a delicious meal regardless of their dietary preferences.

Gluten-free dining has also become more accessible in Australia, with many restaurants and cafes offering gluten-free alternatives to traditional dishes. From gluten-free pasta and pizza to cakes and pastries, those with gluten sensitivities will find plenty of options to enjoy. In addition, many food markets and specialty stores stock gluten-free products, making it easy for travelers to find safe and delicious food options during their stay.

Indulging in Australia's Culinary Diversity

Australia's food and drink scene is a reflection of its multicultural society, offering a rich tapestry of flavors, ingredients, and culinary traditions from around the world. Whether you're indulging in traditional Australian dishes, sipping wine in the country's top wine regions, or enjoying a meal from a food truck in the heart of the city, Australia offers a culinary experience that is both diverse and delicious. With a growing emphasis on sustainability and catering to a range of dietary preferences, Australia's food scene continues to evolve, ensuring that there's something for everyone to enjoy. As you travel through the country, be sure to take the time to savor the flavors of Australia, and let its culinary diversity be a highlight of your journey.

Chapter 8

Immersing Yourself in Australian Culture

Australia's cultural landscape is as vast and varied as the country's geography, offering a unique blend of indigenous traditions, colonial influences, and modern-day multiculturalism. To truly experience Australia, it's essential to immerse yourself in its rich cultural tapestry, engaging with everything from vibrant festivals and events to the country's thriving art and music scenes. This chapter provides a deep dive into Australia's cultural identity, offering insights into its indigenous heritage, tips for attending iconic sporting events, and advice on how to respectfully interact with locals. Whether you're a first-time visitor or a seasoned traveler, Australia's culture offers an unforgettable experience that goes beyond its stunning landscapes.

Australia's Indigenous Heritage: Engaging Respectfully

Australia's indigenous culture is one of the oldest living cultures in the world, dating back more than 60,000 years. The Aboriginal and Torres Strait Islander peoples have a deep connection to the land, with their art, stories, and traditions reflecting their relationship with the natural world. For travelers seeking a meaningful cultural experience, engaging with Australia's indigenous heritage is an essential part of understanding the country's identity.

One of the best ways to immerse yourself in Aboriginal culture is by visiting indigenous art galleries, cultural centers, and museums that showcase traditional and contemporary Aboriginal art. These spaces provide an opportunity to learn about the Dreamtime stories—mythological narratives that explain the creation of the land and its features—through vibrant paintings, carvings, and sculptures. The National Gallery of Australia in Canberra, for example, houses an extensive collection of Aboriginal art, while regional galleries and centers, such as the Tjapukai Aboriginal Cultural Park in Queensland, offer immersive experiences that allow travelers to witness traditional dances, songs, and ceremonies.

Another way to engage with indigenous culture is by joining guided tours led by Aboriginal elders or guides. These tours often focus on the significance of specific landscapes, sacred sites, and natural features, allowing visitors to gain a deeper understanding of Aboriginal spirituality and connection to the land. Experiences such as bush tucker tours, which teach travelers about indigenous food sources, and dot-painting workshops, where you can learn the techniques of traditional Aboriginal art, offer hands-on ways to connect with the culture in a respectful and meaningful manner.

It's important to approach indigenous culture with an open mind and a respectful attitude. Avoid taking photos of sacred sites without permission, and be mindful of cultural sensitivities when engaging in activities that involve indigenous customs and traditions. Many Aboriginal communities welcome visitors who are eager to learn about their culture, but it's crucial to follow their guidance and respect their boundaries to ensure a positive and respectful experience for both travelers and indigenous peoples.

Festivals and Events: Celebrating Australia's Diverse Culture

Australia is home to a vibrant calendar of festivals and events that reflect the country's diverse cultural influences and creative spirit. From major international festivals to smaller, community-based celebrations, there's always something happening that offers a glimpse into Australia's cultural life.

One of the most famous cultural events in Australia is the Sydney Festival, held each January. This multi-disciplinary arts festival features a wide range of performances, including music, dance, theater, and visual arts, with both local and international artists taking part. The festival transforms Sydney into a hub of creativity and celebration, with events taking place in iconic venues such as the Sydney Opera House and outdoor locations around the city.

For music lovers, the Byron Bay Bluesfest is a must-attend event. Held over the Easter long weekend, this festival brings together some of the world's top blues, roots, and rock musicians in the laid-back coastal town of Byron Bay. The festival's relaxed atmosphere and stunning location make it a favorite for both locals and international visitors.

Melbourne, known as Australia's cultural capital, hosts the Melbourne International Comedy Festival, one of the largest comedy festivals in the world. Each year, comedians from around the globe descend on the city to perform stand-up, improv, and sketch comedy, making it a lively and laughter-filled event that attracts both locals and tourists.

In addition to these large-scale events, there are numerous regional festivals that offer a more intimate look at Australia's cultural life. The Darwin Festival, for example, celebrates the Northern Territory's unique blend of indigenous, Asian, and Australian cultures with a mix of music, theater, visual arts, and food events. Meanwhile, the Adelaide Fringe, the largest open-access arts festival in the Southern Hemisphere, brings together performers from a wide range of disciplines, including theater, circus, dance, and cabaret.

Australia's multiculturalism is also reflected in festivals that celebrate the country's diverse immigrant communities. The Lunar New Year celebrations in Sydney's Chinatown and Melbourne's Little Bourke Street are vibrant displays of Chinese culture, featuring dragon and lion dances, traditional performances, and street food. Similarly, Greek festivals, Italian food fairs, and Indian cultural events can be found throughout the country, offering visitors the chance to experience the rich diversity of Australia's immigrant communities.

Sport: The Heartbeat of Australian Culture

Sport is an integral part of Australian culture, with cricket, rugby, and Australian Rules football (AFL) holding a special place in the hearts of many Australians. Attending a live sporting event is a quintessential Australian experience, offering a chance to witness the country's sporting passion firsthand.

Cricket is often referred to as Australia's national sport, and the summer cricket season draws huge crowds to stadiums around the country. Watching a Test match at the iconic Melbourne Cricket Ground (MCG) or a one-day international at the Sydney

Cricket Ground (SCG) is a rite of passage for sports fans. The Boxing Day Test, held annually at the MCG, is one of the most highly anticipated events on the Australian sporting calendar, attracting fans from around the world.

Aussie Rules football, or AFL, is unique to Australia and is one of the country's most popular sports. The AFL season runs from March to September, culminating in the AFL Grand Final, which is held at the MCG and is often compared to the Super Bowl in terms of its cultural significance. Attending an AFL match is a thrilling experience, with the fast-paced action, passionate fans, and electric atmosphere making it a must for any sports enthusiast.

Rugby is also a major sport in Australia, with both Rugby League and Rugby Union having dedicated fan bases. The State of Origin series, a three-game competition between New South Wales and Queensland, is one of the highlights of the Rugby League calendar, while the Bledisloe Cup, contested between Australia and New Zealand, is a key event in Rugby Union.

If you're looking for a more relaxed sporting experience, Australia's beach culture is just as important as its stadium sports. Surfing is a way of life for many Australians, and iconic surf spots like Bondi Beach, Bells Beach, and the Gold Coast attract surfers from around the world. Watching a surfing competition, such as the Rip Curl Pro at Bells Beach, offers a glimpse into the laid-back yet competitive world of Australian surfing.

Art, Music, and Cultural Etiquette

Australia's art and music scenes are thriving, with a wide range of creative expressions reflecting the country's diverse cultural influences. From street art and galleries to live music venues and festivals, Australia offers endless opportunities to engage with its creative spirit.

Melbourne is known for its vibrant street art scene, with laneways like Hosier Lane showcasing ever-changing murals and graffiti by local and international artists. For a more traditional art experience, the National Gallery of Victoria (NGV) in Melbourne and the Art Gallery of New South Wales in Sydney house impressive collections of Australian and international art, while the Museum of Contemporary Art (MCA) in Sydney is dedicated to showcasing cutting-edge contemporary works.

Australia's live music scene is also world-class, with venues ranging from intimate pubs and clubs to large arenas and outdoor festivals. Cities like Sydney, Melbourne, and Brisbane are home to thriving music communities, with artists from a wide range of genres performing regularly. Whether you're into indie rock, electronic, or jazz, you'll find plenty of live music options to suit your tastes.

When interacting with locals, Australians are generally laid-back, friendly, and welcoming. However, there are a few cultural etiquette tips to keep in mind. Australians value humility and dislike pretentiousness, so it's best to avoid boasting or bragging. Punctuality is also appreciated, particularly in business settings, and tipping is not compulsory but is always appreciated for good service.

By immersing yourself in Australia's festivals, arts, music, and sports, and by engaging with its indigenous culture respectfully, you'll gain a deeper understanding of the country's rich and diverse cultural identity. Australia is a land where tradition meets modernity, and by participating in its cultural life, you'll connect with the heart and soul of the nation.

Chapter 9

Sustainable and Responsible Travel in Australia

Australia's stunning natural landscapes, diverse wildlife, and unique cultural heritage are a significant draw for travelers worldwide. However, with tourism comes responsibility, and as visitors, it's essential to be mindful of the impact we leave behind. Sustainable and responsible travel in Australia is about making conscious choices that minimize harm to the environment while contributing positively to local communities and preserving the rich cultural heritage of the country.

Whether you're an eco-conscious traveler or simply want to do your part to protect the beauty of the places you visit, this chapter offers practical, realistic advice on how to make your travels in Australia more sustainable and responsible. By considering your environmental footprint, supporting local businesses, and respecting cultural practices, you can play a part in ensuring that Australia's natural and cultural treasures are preserved for future generations to enjoy.

Eco-Friendly Travel Suggestions: Reducing Your Environmental Impact

Australia's diverse ecosystems—from rainforests to deserts, coral reefs to mountain ranges—are fragile and under increasing pressure from human activity and climate change. Sustainable travel starts with reducing your environmental impact at every stage of your journey. Choosing eco-friendly travel options can help protect these ecosystems while allowing you to experience Australia's beauty without leaving a negative mark.

One of the first steps toward sustainable travel is choosing eco-conscious destinations that prioritize environmental conservation and sustainability. Many of Australia's national parks and eco-resorts have committed to protecting the environment while offering visitors a chance to explore their natural beauty. The Daintree Rainforest in Queensland, for example, is home to eco-lodges that promote sustainable tourism by minimizing their carbon footprint, utilizing renewable energy sources, and supporting local conservation efforts. Similarly, Kangaroo Island in South Australia boasts a wealth of eco-friendly accommodations and activities that allow travelers to connect with nature responsibly.

Staying in green hotels and lodges is another way to ensure your trip is eco-friendly. Look for accommodations with certifications from recognized sustainability organizations, such as Ecotourism Australia or EarthCheck. These accommodations follow strict guidelines to reduce energy consumption, limit water usage, and manage waste responsibly. Many also contribute to wildlife conservation and habitat restoration projects, allowing you to rest easy knowing that your stay supports local environmental efforts.

Minimizing plastic use and reducing waste are crucial aspects of sustainable travel. Australia has taken steps to phase out single-use plastics, with many regions implementing bans on plastic bags, straws, and cutlery. As a traveler, you can do your part by bringing reusable items such as water bottles, shopping bags, and cutlery, reducing your reliance on single-use plastics. Additionally, packing light helps reduce the environmental impact of your transportation, as lighter loads lead to lower fuel consumption in flights and road trips.

Supporting wildlife conservation efforts is another way to travel sustainably. Australia is home to a unique array of wildlife, including kangaroos, koalas, and an astonishing variety of bird species. However, habitat destruction, pollution, and human interference have put many species at risk. Visiting wildlife sanctuaries and conservation centers that prioritize the well-being of animals and their habitats is a great way to enjoy wildlife responsibly. Sanctuaries such as Lone Pine Koala Sanctuary in Brisbane and Healesville Sanctuary in Victoria allow visitors to observe native wildlife up close while supporting important conservation work. By avoiding activities that exploit animals, such as riding captive animals or participating in unethical wildlife encounters, you contribute to the protection of Australia's precious biodiversity.

Supporting Indigenous-Owned Businesses and Ethical Tourism

Australia's indigenous communities have a deep connection to the land, and supporting indigenous-owned businesses is a powerful way to engage in ethical tourism. Whether you're purchasing handmade crafts, joining a cultural tour, or staying at an indigenous-owned lodge, you can directly support Aboriginal and Torres Strait Islander communities. This not only helps sustain their livelihoods but also allows you to gain a more authentic understanding of their culture and traditions.

Many indigenous-owned tourism businesses operate with a focus on sustainability and environmental stewardship. Guided tours led by Aboriginal guides often include education about traditional land management practices and the significance of natural landmarks to indigenous cultures. By participating in these tours, you contribute to the preservation of indigenous knowledge and traditions while enjoying a deeper, more meaningful travel experience.

Another aspect of ethical tourism is ensuring that the experiences you participate in respect local cultures and ecosystems. When choosing tours or activities, look for operators who prioritize sustainability, fair wages, and respect for cultural heritage. For example, consider joining small-group tours that minimize environmental impact and ensure that locals are involved in decision-making processes. Volunteering with conservation projects or community-based initiatives is another way to give back while traveling. Many organizations across Australia offer opportunities for visitors to contribute to environmental restoration, wildlife protection, and community development, allowing you to leave a positive impact on the places you visit.

Volunteering and Engaging in Responsible Travel

One of the most rewarding ways to contribute to sustainability while traveling is by volunteering. Australia offers numerous opportunities for travelers to get involved in conservation, wildlife protection, and community development projects. Whether you're planting trees, helping to rehabilitate wildlife, or assisting with beach clean-ups, volunteering allows you to make a tangible difference during your travels.

For nature lovers, volunteering with organizations like Conservation Volunteers Australia or the Australian Wildlife Conservancy offers the chance to work directly on environmental projects. These projects range from protecting endangered species and restoring habitats to improving the health of Australia's oceans and rivers. Many volunteering programs also provide opportunities for travelers to learn about local ecosystems, giving you a deeper appreciation for the natural beauty you're helping to protect.

In addition to conservation work, travelers can engage in community-based volunteering that supports local economies and cultural preservation. Programs that focus on education, healthcare, and cultural heritage help empower local communities while providing travelers with meaningful, immersive experiences. For example, participating in a cultural exchange program in a remote Aboriginal community allows you to learn about indigenous traditions and lifestyles while contributing to local development efforts.

Responsible travel isn't just about minimizing your environmental impact; it's also about fostering positive relationships with the people and places you visit. Respect for local cultures, traditions, and customs is a cornerstone of responsible tourism. When visiting indigenous communities or remote areas, it's important to follow the guidance of local leaders and avoid behaviors that could be seen as intrusive or disrespectful. This includes asking for permission before taking photos, dressing appropriately for the cultural context, and being mindful of local customs and etiquette.

Leaving a Positive Footprint: Practical Tips for Responsible Travel

Traveling responsibly in Australia is about more than just the big-picture choices—it's also about the small, everyday actions that add up to a more sustainable trip. Simple steps like conserving water, using public transport, and supporting local businesses can make a big difference in reducing your environmental and social impact.

Water conservation is particularly important in Australia, where droughts are common, and water resources can be scarce. Travelers can contribute by taking shorter showers, reusing towels, and being mindful of water usage, especially in remote or drought-prone areas. Similarly, choosing eco-friendly modes of transportation, such as cycling, walking, or using public transport, helps reduce your carbon footprint. When renting a car, consider opting for a hybrid or electric vehicle if available, and aim to carpool or share rides where possible.

Supporting local businesses is another way to leave a positive footprint during your travels. Choosing locally owned accommodations, dining at family-run restaurants, and purchasing souvenirs from local artisans helps keep tourism dollars within the community and supports the livelihoods of those who call Australia home. It also fosters cultural exchange and allows travelers to experience authentic local traditions and flavors.

By making conscious decisions to travel sustainably and responsibly, you'll not only enjoy a more enriching and meaningful travel experience but also help protect Australia's incredible landscapes, wildlife, and cultural heritage for future generations. Every traveler has the power to leave a positive impact—whether by choosing eco-friendly accommodations, supporting indigenous businesses, or volunteering for conservation projects. Through these actions, you can contribute to the preservation of Australia's natural and cultural beauty while creating lasting memories that go beyond the typical tourist experience.

Chapter 10

Family-Friendly Australia

Australia is a destination that offers incredible experiences for travelers of all ages, making it an ideal place for family vacations. With its wide-open spaces, diverse wildlife, and vibrant cities, Australia has something for every member of the family, from young children to adults. Planning a family-friendly trip to Australia means balancing adventure and relaxation, ensuring that both kids and parents can enjoy a stress-free and memorable experience.

Traveling with children often requires additional planning, and this chapter will guide you through the best family-friendly attractions, accommodations, dining options, and practical tips for making the most of your time in Australia. Whether you're exploring the famous wildlife parks, lounging on beautiful beaches, or visiting theme parks, Australia provides endless opportunities for family fun.

Top Family-Friendly Attractions: Zoos, Theme Parks, and Beaches

Australia is known for its diverse and unique wildlife, and no family trip would be complete without visiting some of the country's world-class zoos and wildlife sanctuaries. These attractions not only provide entertainment but also offer educational opportunities for kids to learn about animals they might never encounter elsewhere. The Australia Zoo in Queensland, founded by the late Steve Irwin, is one of the top choices for families. Here, children can marvel at iconic Australian animals like kangaroos, koalas, and crocodiles, and even have the chance to interact with some of the animals through hands-on experiences.

Another must-visit wildlife destination is Taronga Zoo in Sydney. Located just across the harbor, this zoo offers breathtaking views of the city skyline while housing over 4,000 animals from around the world. The zoo features interactive exhibits and keeper talks that engage young minds and inspire a love for conservation. If you're looking for an unforgettable marine experience, Sea World on the Gold Coast offers exciting dolphin and sea lion shows, along with rides and marine animal exhibits that will delight kids of all ages.

For families seeking adventure, Australia's theme parks are a fantastic option. The Gold Coast is home to some of the best theme parks in the country, including Dreamworld, Warner Bros. Movie World, and Wet'n'Wild Water World. Dreamworld, in particular, is ideal for families, as it combines thrilling rides with animal encounters and entertainment suited for younger children. Warner Bros. Movie World brings beloved movie characters to life with exciting rides and live shows that will leave the whole family entertained.

Australia's beautiful beaches are also perfect for family vacations. Bondi Beach in Sydney is well-known for its gentle waves and family-friendly atmosphere, making it a great spot for kids to play in the sand and splash in the water. The Gold Coast also boasts numerous family-friendly beaches such as Surfers Paradise, where lifeguards patrol regularly, and calm waters make it safe for children to swim. Don't forget to explore the quieter beaches, such as Noosa Main Beach in Queensland, which offer a more relaxed environment for families to enjoy together.

For outdoor adventures, the Great Barrier Reef offers a once-in-a-lifetime experience for families. Snorkeling tours are often designed with children in mind, and many tour operators provide safety gear and guidance for young snorkelers. Families can enjoy the vibrant coral reefs and see tropical fish, sea turtles, and other marine life up close.

Kid-Friendly Accommodations and Dining Options

Finding the right accommodation is key to ensuring a smooth and enjoyable family vacation. Australia offers a wide range of family-friendly accommodations, from hotels with kids' clubs and swimming pools to self-catered apartments that provide more space for families to spread out. Many hotels and resorts across Australia cater specifically to families, offering amenities such as babysitting services, children's menus, and playgrounds.

On the Gold Coast, resorts like Paradise Resort are designed with families in mind. The resort features water parks, daily activities for kids, and entertainment that will keep children engaged while parents relax. Similarly, in Sydney, the Four

Seasons Hotel offers family packages that include children's amenities and access to kid-friendly attractions.

Camping and holiday parks are another popular accommodation option for families in Australia. Parks such as Big4 Holiday Parks are scattered across the country and are specifically tailored to families, offering facilities like playgrounds, swimming pools, and even mini-golf courses. Staying in a holiday park allows families to experience the great outdoors while having access to essential amenities, creating a balance between adventure and comfort.

When it comes to dining, Australia offers a variety of options to satisfy even the pickiest eaters. Many family-friendly restaurants provide special kids' menus with healthy and delicious choices, ensuring that dining out is a breeze. Australian pubs, known as "hotels," often serve up classic Aussie meals like fish and chips, burgers, and steaks, which are typically family-friendly and offer a casual dining experience. In addition, many pubs have outdoor play areas, so children can entertain themselves while waiting for their meals.
For more casual dining, food trucks and markets are excellent options. Food markets, such as the

Queen Victoria Market in Melbourne or the Sydney Fish Market, provide an array of international cuisines and local treats that kids will love. The vibrant atmosphere of these markets makes them a fun and affordable dining experience for families, and the variety of foods means there's something for everyone, from pizza and noodles to fresh fruit and smoothies.

Practical Tips for Stress-Free Family Travel

Traveling with children can be challenging, but with the right planning and preparation, it can also be incredibly rewarding. One of the most important factors to consider is transportation. Australia's cities offer a variety of transportation options that are easy to navigate with children. In major cities like Sydney, Melbourne, and Brisbane, public transportation is reliable and family-friendly. Buses, trains, and ferries are equipped with accessible features, such as ramps and priority seating for families with strollers.

Renting a car is another convenient option, especially when traveling between destinations or exploring more remote areas. Car rental companies in Australia offer a range of vehicle sizes to accommodate families, and car seats for young children can be added to your rental. When driving long distances, be sure to plan regular stops to let children stretch their legs and avoid restlessness.

Keeping children entertained during long flights or car journeys is essential for a stress-free trip. Bringing along a selection of books, games, or electronic devices can help pass the time. Many airlines provide in-flight entertainment systems with kid-friendly movies and games, and some airlines even offer special children's meal options.

When it comes to packing, ensure you're prepared for Australia's varying climates. If you're traveling to multiple regions, you may experience different weather conditions, so pack accordingly. For warm destinations like the Gold Coast, light clothing, sunscreen, and hats are essential. If your trip includes cooler regions such as Tasmania, pack warmer layers for chilly mornings and evenings.

To avoid unexpected stress, plan your itinerary with a balance of activity and downtime. Children can become easily overwhelmed if the schedule is too packed, so be sure to include time for rest and relaxation. Whether it's spending a day lounging at the beach or enjoying a leisurely afternoon in a park, allowing time for children to recharge will make the vacation more enjoyable for everyone.

Activities for Both Parents and Children

A successful family vacation is one where both parents and children can have fun together. Australia offers a wealth of activities that appeal to all ages, allowing families to create shared memories while also enjoying moments of relaxation. Exploring the outdoors is one of the best ways to bond as a family in Australia. National parks such as the Blue Mountains near Sydney or Kakadu National Park in the Northern Territory offer hiking trails that cater to various skill levels, making them accessible to families with young children.

Outdoor adventures such as whale watching, boat tours, or snorkeling are great ways for families to experience Australia's natural beauty together. On the Sunshine Coast, family-friendly boat tours offer the chance to spot dolphins, whales, and even sea turtles. These tours are often designed with kids in mind, providing engaging commentary and activities to keep young travelers entertained.

Museums and interactive exhibits are another excellent option for families. Many Australian cities boast child-friendly museums that provide hands-on learning experiences. The Australian Museum in Sydney, for example, features interactive exhibits on natural history and Australian wildlife that are designed to capture children's curiosity. Similarly, the Melbourne Museum offers a dedicated children's gallery where kids can explore and learn through play.

Family vacations are about creating lasting memories, and Australia provides endless opportunities for families to enjoy meaningful experiences together. Whether it's exploring the vibrant cities, connecting with nature, or simply enjoying a relaxed day at the beach, Australia has something for everyone, making it the perfect destination for a family adventure. With the right planning and an open spirit, you'll be able to create a trip that delights both parents and children alike, ensuring a vacation full of joy, discovery, and togetherness.

Chapter 11

Essential Practical Tips for Travelers

Traveling to Australia is an incredible adventure, but like any trip, it comes with challenges that can be minimized with the right preparation. This chapter serves as your comprehensive guide to navigating the practicalities of travel in Australia. From staying safe and healthy to ensuring you stay connected and have access to essential services, this section will address the key concerns that travelers commonly face. Equipped with this knowledge, you'll be better prepared to fully enjoy your journey across this vast and diverse country.

Staying Safe in Cities, the Outback, and During Outdoor Activities

Australia is known for being a safe destination for travelers, but it's still important to take basic precautions, particularly when visiting unfamiliar places or engaging in adventurous activities. In major cities like Sydney, Melbourne, and Brisbane, crime rates are relatively low, but it's always wise to exercise general safety measures. Keep an eye on your belongings, especially in crowded areas, and avoid walking alone at night in less populated neighborhoods. The same precautions apply to public transport—stay alert and aware of your surroundings, especially during late hours.

When venturing into the Australian outback or more remote areas, the safety landscape changes. The vast, isolated nature of these regions presents unique risks, including extreme weather conditions, rough terrain, and limited access to services. Before setting out, always inform someone of your travel plans, particularly if you'll be hiking or driving long distances in remote areas. Carry plenty of water, especially during hot weather, and make sure your vehicle is well-maintained with a full tank of fuel. Keep an emergency kit in your car, complete with first-aid supplies, a spare tire, extra fuel, and enough food and water to last several days, should you become stranded.

When engaging in outdoor activities, safety becomes paramount. Australia's beaches, national parks, and adventure sports can be thrilling but also hazardous if not approached with care. Always follow posted signs at beaches regarding swimming conditions, and never swim outside designated areas. Australian beaches are patrolled by lifeguards, and it's important to heed their advice, especially in areas where dangerous currents (rips) may be present. In the bush or national parks, stay on marked trails to avoid getting lost and be mindful of wildlife, such as snakes or spiders, which can be encountered in more isolated areas.

Health Precautions and Emergency Contacts

Traveling to Australia typically doesn't require any vaccinations beyond routine immunizations, but it's always a good idea to check with your healthcare provider for recommendations based on your personal health. Travelers coming from countries where yellow fever is present may need to show proof of vaccination upon entering Australia. If you're planning to explore remote regions or engage in specific outdoor activities, ensure your tetanus vaccinations are up to date, and consider protection against mosquito-borne diseases like dengue fever, especially in the tropical north.

While Australia has an excellent healthcare system, it's important to note that healthcare can be costly for non-residents. Travel insurance is a must for any trip to Australia, covering not only health-related emergencies but also trip interruptions, lost baggage, and any accidents during adventurous activities. Make sure your insurance policy includes coverage for high-risk activities such as scuba diving, skydiving, or hiking, depending on your itinerary.

Australia's emergency number is 000, and this should be used for urgent police, fire, or medical assistance. For non-emergency medical help, local clinics and hospitals are available in most cities and towns. In rural areas, however, medical services can be scarce, so it's important to carry a well-stocked first-aid kit and know basic first-aid procedures. Pharmacies are widespread across the country, and pharmacists can often provide advice for minor health concerns, such as allergies, insect bites, or common colds.

Staying Connected: Wi-Fi, Mobile Services, and Useful Apps

Staying connected while traveling in Australia is generally easy, especially in urban areas. Most hotels, cafes, and public spaces offer free Wi-Fi, though the quality and speed can vary. If you need reliable internet access throughout your trip, consider purchasing a local SIM card with a data plan. Major mobile providers such as Telstra, Optus, and Vodafone offer prepaid SIM cards that are widely available at airports, convenience stores, and mobile phone shops. These SIM cards can be used for both calls and data, allowing you to stay connected wherever there's coverage.

While mobile reception in cities and towns is excellent, it can be patchy or non-existent in more remote regions, such as the outback or parts of the national parks. If you're planning an extended trip to these areas, consider investing in a satellite phone or, at the very least, ensure that you have a good offline map app downloaded onto your phone before heading into areas without coverage.

Australia is also home to a number of useful travel apps that can enhance your journey. Some popular apps include "TripView" for public transport in Sydney, "GoCatch" for ride-sharing, and "FuelMap Australia" to help you locate the nearest petrol stations. For outdoor enthusiasts, apps like "Wikicamps Australia" provide valuable information on campsites and facilities across the country, while "First Aid by Australian Red Cross" can be a helpful tool in case of medical emergencies.

Money Matters: Exchanging Currency and Handling Finances

Australia's currency is the Australian dollar (AUD), and it's advisable to carry some cash, especially when traveling to rural areas or small towns where card payments may not always be accepted. In major cities, card payments are widely accepted, and ATMs are easily accessible. Visa and Mastercard are the most commonly accepted credit cards, though American Express is also accepted at many establishments.

If you need to exchange currency, you can do so at airports, major hotels, banks, or currency exchange offices. However, be aware that airport exchange rates are often less favorable than those found elsewhere. ATMs often provide the best exchange rates, so withdrawing local currency using your debit card can be an efficient option. Just be sure to inform your bank before traveling to avoid any blocks on your account for suspicious activity.

Mobile payment options like Apple Pay and Google Pay are also gaining popularity in Australia, so you may find it convenient to use these services for contactless payments. If you're planning to stay for an extended period, it may be worthwhile opening an Australian bank account to avoid international transaction fees.

Useful Travel Apps and Staying Organized

In addition to apps for transport and communication, there are several travel apps that can help you stay organized and make the most of your time in Australia. Apps like "Google Maps" or "Citymapper" are indispensable for navigating cities and finding attractions, while "Rome2Rio" can help you compare transport options between different locations, whether you're driving, flying, or taking public transport.

For budgeting and keeping track of expenses, "Trail Wallet" is an excellent app that allows you to set a daily budget and monitor your spending. Another useful app is "PackPoint," which creates customized packing lists based on your destination, the length of your stay, and the activities you have planned. If you're a foodie, apps like "Zomato" or "The Fork" can help you discover the best restaurants and read reviews before deciding where to eat.

Traveling can sometimes throw unexpected challenges your way, but with careful planning and the right tools at your disposal, these challenges can be minimized. Having a well-organized itinerary, staying informed about the local environment, and taking the necessary precautions will allow you to focus on what truly matters—enjoying the incredible experiences Australia has to offer.

Finally, planning for the practical aspects of travel is just as important as choosing where to go and what to see. With this chapter's guidance, you'll be well-prepared to navigate the ins and outs of traveling in Australia. By staying safe, informed, and connected, you can focus on making unforgettable memories while exploring the beauty and wonder of this remarkable country. With the right balance of preparation and spontaneity, your journey through Australia will be as smooth and enjoyable as it is adventurous.

Chapter 12

Suggested Itineraries for Every Traveler

Whether you're a first-time visitor eager to see Australia's iconic landmarks, a backpacker looking for adventure on a budget, a family in search of memorable moments, or a luxury traveler yearning for indulgence, this chapter provides well-crafted itineraries tailored to suit your style. Traveling across Australia can be a transformative experience, but with so much to explore, it's easy to feel overwhelmed by the choices. To help, we've created a series of diverse itineraries that ensure you make the most of your time, no matter your preferences or budget.

Classic Two-Week Itinerary for First-Time Visitors

Australia's vastness can be intimidating for first-time visitors, but this classic two-week itinerary is designed to provide a perfect introduction. It covers the must-see attractions, offering a mix of city life, nature, and cultural experiences. Begin your journey in Sydney, exploring the world-famous Sydney Opera House, the Harbour Bridge, and Bondi Beach. Spend two days wandering through the city's vibrant neighborhoods, taking a day trip to the Blue Mountains for a taste of Australia's rugged wilderness.

Next, fly to Cairns to experience the Great Barrier Reef, one of the natural wonders of the world. Spend a few days diving or snorkeling among the coral reefs, followed by an inland journey to the Daintree Rainforest, where you'll encounter unique wildlife and awe-inspiring landscapes. After soaking up the tropical atmosphere, head to the Northern Territory to experience the raw beauty of Uluru. Watching the sunset over the red rock formation is a once-in-a-lifetime experience that will leave you spellbound. Spend two days exploring the surrounding desert landscapes and learning about the area's deep Aboriginal significance.

End your journey in Melbourne, Australia's cultural capital. Spend your last few days visiting the city's iconic laneways, indulging in the diverse food scene, and experiencing the dynamic art galleries and museums. Be sure to take a day trip along the Great Ocean Road to marvel at the dramatic coastline and the Twelve Apostles. With this well-balanced itinerary, you'll have a perfect mix of Australia's urban charm, natural wonders, and cultural richness.

Budget-Friendly Backpacker Route

Australia is known for its adventurous spirit, and backpackers from all over the world flock here for the thrill of the open road, the friendly locals, and the natural beauty. This budget-friendly route is designed for those who want to see the best of Australia without breaking the bank. Start in Brisbane, where you can explore the city's cultural sites and beaches while staying in affordable hostels. Brisbane is a great launching point for the East Coast road trip—one of the most popular backpacker routes in Australia.

Head north along the coast to the Sunshine Coast and Noosa, where you can enjoy pristine beaches, budget-friendly outdoor activities, and relaxed vibes. Continue up to Airlie Beach, the gateway to the Whitsunday Islands. Camping on the islands or staying in budget-friendly lodges will allow you to experience paradise without overspending. Be sure to take advantage of the free activities like hiking, swimming, and snorkeling in the surrounding national parks.

Further north, Cairns offers budget accommodation and the chance to explore the Great Barrier Reef on a budget. Many affordable tours cater to backpackers, providing snorkeling or diving adventures at a fraction of the cost. After Cairns, fly west to Alice Springs to explore the Outback. Uluru and Kings Canyon are major highlights here, and with camping options and guided tours, you can experience the Outback's magic without straining your budget. End your trip in Adelaide, where you can enjoy the beach and lively markets before flying home. This route promises adventure, stunning landscapes, and authentic experiences on a budget.

Luxury Experience Itinerary

For travelers who want to indulge in luxury while exploring Australia, this itinerary focuses on high-end accommodations, exclusive experiences, and gourmet dining. Start your journey in Sydney, staying at one of the city's top hotels overlooking

Sydney Harbour. Begin your luxury experience with a private yacht tour of the harbor, followed by dinner at a world-class restaurant such as Quay or Bennelong. Spend your days exploring the city's top attractions, but with a twist—book private tours of the Sydney Opera House or VIP experiences at the city's museums and galleries.

Next, fly to Tasmania, one of Australia's most serene and untouched destinations. Stay at one of Tasmania's luxury eco-lodges, such as Saffire Freycinet, where you'll be pampered with personalized service and gourmet cuisine. Explore the island's beautiful landscapes on private guided hikes or exclusive wildlife tours, and end your days enjoying local Tasmanian wine and food.

Continue your journey by flying to the Barossa Valley, Australia's premier wine region. Indulge in a luxury wine-tasting experience, complete with vineyard tours, gourmet meals, and stays in boutique hotels. Enjoy exclusive access to some of the world's best vineyards, and take in the scenic beauty of rolling hills and lush vineyards.

Finally, fly to the Great Barrier Reef for the ultimate luxury escape. Stay at one of the exclusive resorts on Lizard Island or Hayman Island, where you can experience the reef's underwater wonders in private tours, or enjoy helicopter rides over the breathtaking coral formations. Finish your trip with a relaxing spa day, complete with personalized treatments designed to refresh and rejuvenate you after your adventure.

Family-Focused Adventure

Australia is an ideal destination for families, offering a wealth of kid-friendly activities and accommodations. This family-focused itinerary is designed to keep both parents and children entertained and stress-free. Begin in Sydney, where your family can enjoy the Taronga Zoo, the SEA LIFE Sydney Aquarium, and Luna Park amusement park. Spend a day at Bondi Beach, where kids can swim and play in the sand, while parents relax by the water.

After Sydney, head to the Gold Coast, known for its famous theme parks. Spend a few days exploring Dreamworld, Warner Bros. Movie World, and Sea World, where the whole family can enjoy rides, shows, and wildlife encounters. For a more relaxed experience, take the family to the nearby

Currumbin Wildlife Sanctuary, where children can get up close to kangaroos and koalas.

Next, fly to Cairns, where family-friendly attractions include the Cairns Esplanade Lagoon—a free outdoor pool perfect for kids—and family snorkeling tours at the Great Barrier Reef. If your children enjoy nature, take them on a guided tour of the nearby rainforests, where they'll learn about Australia's unique wildlife and ecosystems.

End your family adventure in Melbourne, where the Melbourne Zoo, Scienceworks museum, and kid-friendly activities along the Yarra River offer plenty of fun. With a mix of thrilling attractions, wildlife experiences, and family-oriented accommodations, this itinerary ensures that your family will leave Australia with countless memories.

Eco-Tourism Itinerary

For eco-conscious travelers, Australia offers a wealth of sustainable travel options that allow you to explore the country's natural beauty while minimizing your environmental impact. Begin your eco-tourism journey in the Daintree Rainforest, staying at eco-friendly lodges that are committed to conservation and sustainability. Take guided nature walks with local experts, learning about the delicate ecosystem and how to protect it.

From there, head to Kangaroo Island, a paradise for wildlife lovers. Stay at an eco-lodge that supports local conservation efforts, and spend your days exploring the island's pristine beaches, forests, and wildlife sanctuaries. Watch sea lions bask on the beaches, spot koalas in their natural habitat, and explore the island's remarkable rock formations, all while supporting sustainable tourism initiatives.

Fly to the Whitsunday Islands, where you can take part in eco-friendly snorkeling or diving tours that prioritize the preservation of the Great Barrier Reef. Many local operators offer carbon-neutral tours that focus on reef conservation. Stay at a resort that implements green practices, such as using solar power and reducing plastic waste.

Conclude your eco-tourism adventure in Tasmania, staying at one of the island's many eco-resorts. Explore Tasmania's national parks, such as Cradle Mountain or Freycinet National Park, while taking care to respect the natural environment. Participate in guided conservation activities, such as tree planting or wildlife tracking, to give back to the environment and help preserve Australia's natural beauty for future generations.

Each of these itineraries is designed to provide a tailored experience that caters to different travel styles and preferences. Whether you're seeking luxury, adventure, budget-conscious exploration, family-friendly activities, or eco-tourism, Australia has something for every traveler. These itineraries offer the perfect blend of structure and flexibility, ensuring you can enjoy Australia in a way that suits your unique travel needs.

Appendix

The appendix is designed to serve as a practical and easy-to-navigate resource for travelers, offering essential tools and insights to enhance your trip to Australia. Whether you're in need of booking websites, useful apps, emergency contacts, or a quick reference for Australian slang, this section will help ensure a smooth and stress-free journey. It also provides further reading recommendations for travelers who wish to delve deeper into Australia's rich history, culture, and nature.

Key Travel Information and Booking Resources

When planning a trip to Australia, having access to reliable and comprehensive booking resources is crucial. There are numerous websites that offer great deals on flights, accommodations, tours, and transportation. Websites like Skyscanner, Expedia, and Kayak can be used for booking flights and comparing prices, while Booking.com and Airbnb provide a wide range of accommodations, from budget-friendly options to luxurious stays. For car rentals, services such as Hertz, Avis, and Budget offer convenient options for exploring Australia by road. If you prefer train travel, the Great Southern Rail site provides schedules and booking options for iconic Australian trains like The Ghan and the Indian Pacific.

In addition to websites, apps like Rome2Rio, which helps travelers find the best way to get from one place to another, or TripIt, which helps organize travel plans, are invaluable tools to streamline your trip. Australia also has local rideshare apps such as Uber and Ola that are widely available in cities, making transportation easy and efficient.

Emergency Contacts and Health Resources

Having emergency contacts readily available is essential for peace of mind while traveling. Australia is a safe country, but accidents and emergencies can happen, so it's important to know how to reach the right services. Dial 000 in the event of a medical, fire, or police emergency. For non-emergency medical assistance, call Health

Direct at **1800 022 222**, which is available 24/7 for health advice.

Travelers should also be aware of local hospitals or medical centers in the areas they plan to visit. In cities, public hospitals are well-equipped for emergencies and care, while in more remote areas, the Royal Flying Doctor Service provides medical aid to outback regions. It's highly recommended to have travel insurance that covers medical emergencies, especially if you plan on engaging in outdoor or adventure activities like diving or hiking in remote areas.

Travel Checklist

Packing for a trip to Australia requires careful planning to ensure you're well-prepared for the variety of climates and activities. Here's a quick checklist of essentials:

Travel Documents: Passport, visas, flight confirmations, insurance details, and copies of all documents.
Clothing: Light, breathable clothing for warm days; layers for cooler nights; a jacket for winter

months; swimwear; comfortable walking shoes; and a hat for sun protection.

Toiletries: Sunscreen (SPF 50+), insect repellent, personal care items, and any prescription medications.

Electronics: Chargers, a power bank, travel adapters (Australia uses Type I plugs), and a camera for capturing the beauty of the landscape.

Eco-friendly gear: Reusable water bottles, reusable shopping bags, and biodegradable toiletries to reduce your environmental impact.

First Aid Kit: Basic first-aid supplies, such as bandages, antiseptic cream, and over-the-counter medications for pain, allergies, or stomach issues.

Travel Guides and Maps: A physical map or guidebook can be helpful in areas with limited cell service.

Currency and Tipping Guide

Australia's currency is the Australian Dollar (AUD). It's easy to exchange foreign currency at airports, banks, and exchange services in most major cities. Credit cards are widely accepted, and ATMs are readily available in cities and towns. For travelers heading into more remote areas, it's a good idea to carry some cash, as ATMs may be less frequent, and smaller establishments may not accept cards.

Tipping is not as customary in Australia as it is in some other countries, but it is appreciated for excellent service. In restaurants, rounding up the bill or leaving a small tip (around 10%) is considered generous but not obligatory. Taxi drivers, hotel staff, and baristas do not expect tips, but rounding up the fare or leaving a few dollars for exceptional service is a kind gesture.

Common Australian Slang and Phrases

Understanding a few key Australian slang terms and phrases can make your experience more enjoyable and help you connect with the locals. Australians are known for their relaxed and informal approach to language, so it's helpful to be familiar with some common terms:

G'day – Hello
Arvo – Afternoon
Brekkie – Breakfast
Fair dinkum – Genuine, honest
Mate – Friend (used universally for both men and women)

No worries – It's okay; don't worry about it
Servo – Gas station
Bogan – An unsophisticated person (similar to "redneck" in the U.S.)
Thongs – Flip-flops
By familiarizing yourself with these phrases, you'll feel more at ease when conversing with locals and navigating Australian culture.

In conclusion, this appendix serves as a valuable resource to complement your travels across Australia. Whether you need booking websites, emergency contacts, or insight into local slang, this section provides everything you need for a safe, informed, and enjoyable journey. Additionally, the recommended reading offers a deeper dive into Australia's history, culture, and environment for those who wish to expand their knowledge before or during their trip. Use this appendix to feel well-prepared and confident as you embark on your Australian adventure.

Made in the USA
Las Vegas, NV
07 January 2025

15999025R00068